Author: Marva Goins
Illustrations: Taranggana

ISBN: 978- 1-7322838-0-0

This book was printed in the United States of America

Library of Congress Control Number : 2018910659

Acknowledgement

Through effort and a process I would like to thank the following people:

Renaee Smith, IABX founder and CEBP, for her unwavering guidance, suggestions, attitude and constant support during my first attempt at writing a children's book.

Sheila Casey for numerous typing of the initial manuscript and editing .

My peers in the "Group", every Monday evening, who cheered all of us on attempting this fantastic journey.

Zaaire
and
The Brushing
Teeth Lesson

One day a group of stuffed animals named Pinky Pig, Fluffy Rabbit, Spiky Porcupine, Pop Hop the Frog and Sluggy Turtle got together in the living room to discuss a problem Zaaire, a three year old child, was having at home.

Since they all lived with him, they saw him and played with him every day. They have seen some of his behavior and thought they could help.

Pinky Pig started first. "I overheard his Aunt tell him -'Brush your teeth, put the toothbrush in your mouth.'" Zaaire just stared at the toothbrush then wiggled the brush around near his mouth, but not in his mouth.

He stood there looking at the toothbrush for about sixty seconds. Tick-tock, tick-tock, tick-tock. The animals all look at each other and hold a meeting. They each decide that they will think of something to help Zaaire.

12
1
2
3
4
5
6
7
8
9
10
11

Fluffy Rabbit noticed the time.
"It's 8:00 pm. Let's go to the bathroom with Zaaire."
The animals all speak in a chorus.
"Zaaire, are you ready to brush your teeth?"
Zaaire looks at them and shaking his head "no." "We are here to help you!"
Zaaire says, "Okay."

Pop Hop the Frog says,
"Zoom the toothbrush like a flying airplane, zoom the toothbrush into your mouth."
Pop Hop makes a motion. Zaaire follows and propels the toothbrush right into his mouth. Smiling he says, "I can do it!"

Pinky Pig says,
"Maybe Zaaire could start brushing his teeth to a song:

Brusha, Brusha
Brush your teeth
Get them nice and clean.
You want your smile
to look the best
You want your teeth
to gleam

Zaaire moves the toothbrush, shaking
his head back and forth, humming the tune.
The animals are singing the song.

Fluffy Rabbit suggests,
Brusha, brusha,
Brush your teeth
Back teeth, front teeth
Upside down,
Brusha, Brusha around
and around

Spiky porcupine says. Turn your brush upside down. Right side. Left side. now all around and up and down.

Now Zaaire is feeling good. he is moving his body from side to side.

Sluggy Turtle called out, "

Brusha, brusha, brush your teeth
So they're nice and white
Brusha, brusha, brush your teeth
So they shine in the light.

Finally, Zaaire's teeth are clean!!
Zaaire looks in the bathroom mirror, shows a big smile and white teeth.

He runs down the stairs to show his aunt with the animals right behind him.

She smiles and says.
"Yeah Such bright teeth. you did a great job Zaaire."
Your animal friends really helped you."
He is happy! He turns around and says.

"Thank you my friends, now I love to brush my teeth. The animals look at each other and smile. They are so glad that they could help Zaaire, a friend. They were content.

www.ingramcontent.com/pod-product-compliance
Lightning Source LLC
LaVergne TN
LVHW052303100826
845147LV00001B/127